The Train

Caroline Sewell

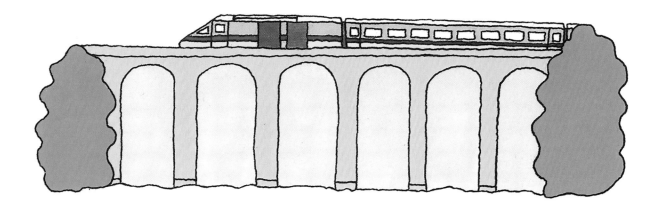

Illustrated by Tony Wells

Conran Octopus

David and his mum are going by train to see Granny.

'Which platform does our train go from?' asks mum, as she buys their tickets.

'Number 2,' says the man in the ticket office.

In the sheds, people are hard at work getting the train ready.

The foreman and his workmates clean the inside of the carriages. Big rollers clean the outside.

The driver stops the engine by the fuel pump. The engine must be filled with diesel fuel before it starts its journey. The dial on the pump shows when the tank is full.

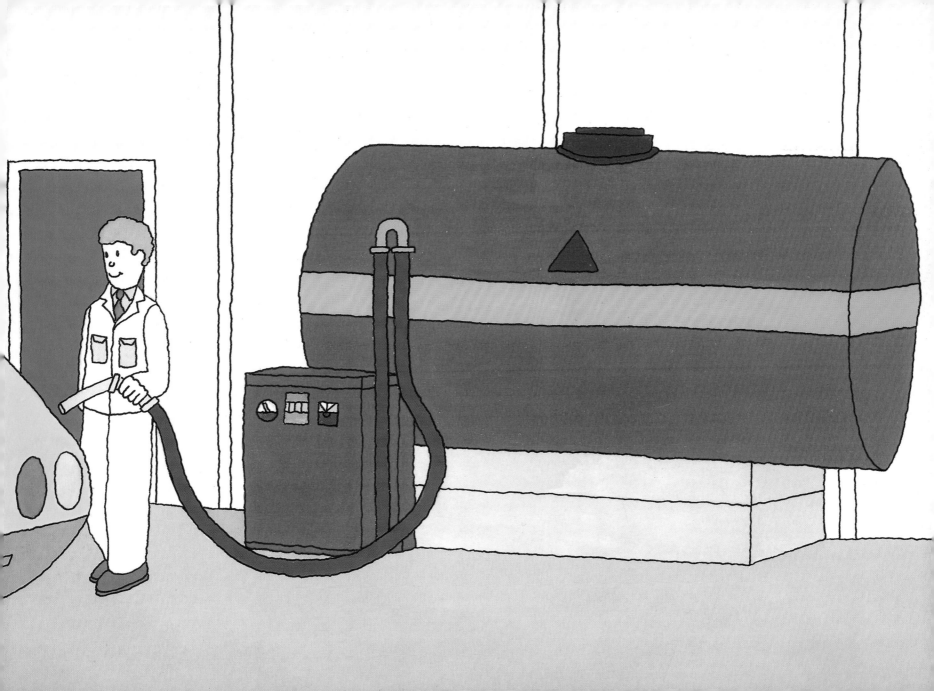

'Hurry up now,' says the man at the gate, as he punches their tickets.

'Look, look, the train is coming!' shouts David.

He watches the train arrive at the platform.

Everyone boards the train and settles down for the journey. The doors are shut and the signal is green, which means they can go. The guard blows his whistle. They're off.

The train picks up speed as it leaves town. Soon David can see fields.

'When I went on my first train journey, we had a steam engine,' says mum. 'The train was fuelled by coal and clouds of smoke poured out of the chimney.'

The train passes over a level crossing. David can see a line of cars waiting to pass. The signalman waves to him and David waves back.

'They all had to stop for us!' says David, as the train rushes on.

'Tickets please,' calls the ticket inspector down the carriage. David shows him his ticket.

A waitress comes down the aisle with sandwiches and drinks. David chooses what he wants. His mum buys a cup of tea.

They can feel the train slowing down. David looks out of the window. There are men working on the line.

'They're checking the points,' says mum. 'The points control which way the train goes.'

Soon they're off again, speeding along.
There's a tunnel ahead. The driver sounds the horn.
'It won't be long now before we reach Granny's,'
says mum, 'we'd better pack up and put our coats on.'
'I can't wait for my next train journey,' says David.

First published 1987 in Great Britain by
Conran Octopus Limited
28-32 Shelton Street London WC2 9PH
Copyright © Conran Octopus Limited

Designed by Heather Garioch
Printed in Spain by
Cayfosa, Barcelona
Dep. Leg. B-24566-1987
ISBN 1 85029 118 7